Pray in This Way

by Dorothy Fay Richards
illustrated by
Jenny Williams

Published by The Dandelion House
A Division of The Child's World

for distribution by **VICTOR**
BOOKS a division of SP Publications, Inc.
WHEATON. ILLINOIS 60187

Offices also in
Whitby, Ontario, Canada
Amersham-on-the-Hill, Bucks, England

Published by The Dandelion House, A Division of The Child's World, Inc.
© 1983 SP Publications, Inc. All rights reserved. Printed in U.S.A.

A Book for Competent Readers.

Library of Congress Cataloging in Publication Data

Richards, Dorothy Fay
  Pray in this way.

  Summary: Discusses reasons why we pray and retells
Bible stories in which prayer plays an important part.
    1. Prayer—Juvenile literature.   [1. Prayer.   2. Bible
stories]   I. Williams, Jenny, ill.   II. Title.
BV212.R48   1983   248.3'2   83-7342
ISBN 0-89693-215-X

1 2 3 4 5 6 7 8 9 10 11 12 R 90 89 88 87 86 85 84 83

Pray in This Way

Why Should I Pray?

HELP!

The world is very big. You and I are very little.

We need Someone bigger and stronger and wiser than we are to help us. Someone bigger and stronger and wiser than our parents and teachers.

That Someone is God.

We talk to God for many reasons. Talking to God is called prayer.

God is always listening, waiting for us to talk to Him.

Sometimes we are very happy about something. We want to tell God this. That is one reason to pray.

• The sun just came out from behind a black cloud!

• Your friend who moved away called to say hi.

• Your dog had five puppies!

Why would you tell God these things? Because you want to. And because God loves you and is always listening, waiting for you to talk to Him.

Other times, we are sad about something. We want to tell God this, too.

• Your sister has the flu and you feel bad, too.

• You feel lonesome or hurt.

• You think you will never be old enough to do anything!

Why would you tell God these things? Because you want to. And because God loves you and can help you.

Sometimes we pray because we need forgiveness. (We tell others we are sorry. Gods wants to know when we are sorry, too.) God will always forgive us when we ask Him.

We pray because we need something. We need help or someone we know needs help.

We pray because the Bible tells us God wants us to talk to Him. He made us and wants to keep in touch! He is always listening, waiting for us to talk to Him.

"You will pray to him, and he will hear you"
—Job 22:27. (TLB)

What should I pray about?

There are lots of reasons to pray. And there are lots of things to pray about!

Some days, everything goes so right we feel like saying, "Thank You, God!" at the end of the day. (And other days, when things go partly right and partly wrong, there are still many things to thank God for.)

Pray about all the things for which you are thankful.

- "Thank You, God, for the world and everything in it."

- "Thank You for the sun and moon and wind and rain."

"In every thing give thanks"—
1 Thess. 5:18. (KJV)

8

● "Thank You for my city, my street, and a place to live."

● "Thank You for all the people who love me."

● "Thank You for loving me. Thank You for Jesus."

9

Other days, everything goes wrong. You think, "Nobody likes me. I don't have any friends. There is nothing to do."

Cheer up! Somebody besides you thought like that. His name was Elijah. He felt so alone, he went into the wilderness—where he really *was* alone! He prayed to God in a cave. And God said to Elijah: "What are you doing here? You have seven thousand friends! Get up and get going!"

Just like Elijah, you can pray about feeling lonely or sad: "God help me find friends. And help me be a good friend to others." And God will help you!

Another time, you might want or need something. But you think you will never have it. This is what happened to Hannah.

Hannah wanted a child more than anything. But the older she got, the more she thought, "I will live and die without children."

Finally, Hannah went to God's house to pray about it. And after awhile, Hannah had a child! Her child, Samuel, loved God and worked for Him.

Just like Hannah, you can pray about things you want. Sometimes God will say, "Yes." Sometimes He will say, "No." Sometimes He will say, "Wait."

Have you ever been really afraid? Maybe it was in a storm. Or in the dark. What did you do?

One time a man named Paul, and his friend Silas, were put in prison for preaching about Jesus. They were beaten and put into a deep dungeon.

Did they cry out and beg not to be killed? Were they afraid of what would happen next?—No.

There, in the dungeon, Paul and Silas sang and prayed to God. And that night, because of Paul and Silas, the jailkeeper and his family believed in Jesus.

Just like Paul and Silas, you can pray about being afraid: ''God, help me not to be afraid, no matter what happens. I know You are with me. Help me to remember this.''

''They that know your name will put their trust in you''—Psalm 9:10.
(Paraphrased)

Uh-oh!

You have done something *so bad* you want to hide under your bed—way under! Nothing will help you feel better, ever.

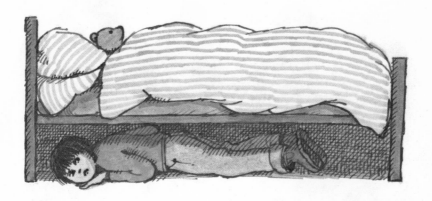

This happened to Peter, a close friend of Jesus. Jesus said, "Bad things are going to happen to Me, and all of you will leave Me."

Peter said, "I will never leave You!"

But Peter did. Afterwards, he remembered what Jesus had said. And Peter was ashamed.

But later, Jesus forgave Peter. Peter felt so much better.

Just like Peter, you can be forgiven. You can pray, "God, forgive me for the wrong things I did today. Thank You for forgiving me. Thank You for giving me a fresh start."

"You, Lord, are good and ready to forgive"—Psalm 86:5.
(Paraphrased)

Sometimes we forget to pray. Instead, we worry.

Once Peter was put in prison for preaching about Jesus. Peter did not worry. He fell asleep in the prison.

Peter's friends thought they might never see him again. Did they say—"Oh no! What will we do? We'll never see Peter again"?—No.

Peter's friends met together to pray. The prayer meeting lasted day and night!

While Peter's friends were praying, an angel came and led Peter out of prison!

Just like Peter's friends, instead of worrying, you can pray: "God, thank You for taking care of those who love You. Help me do what I can do and leave the rest to You. I know You will do what is best."

When should we pray?

In some of our Bible stories, people prayed at noon or at three o'clock, or, as Daniel did, three times in a day. We know God is listening and waiting for us to talk to Him anytime, anyplace.

Here are some times you may want to pray.

✳ Before you go to sleep at night.

✳ When you wake up in the morning.

✱ When you have a special need—
a danger,
a duty,
a hard-thing-to-do.

✱ When you want to ask God's forgiveness.

✱ When you have been reading a Bible story.

✱ When you want to thank or praise God.

❋ At mealtimes.

There are no "have-to" words to say, no "have-to" times to pray. God wants us to talk to Him in our own words—anytime, anyplace.

Should we kneel? That is not important. The important thing is that we pray honestly, not just for others to see.

Jesus told about two men who went into the temple to pray. One man thought he was very good. He said, "Look at me, God! I am so good I fast twice a week. I give a tenth of all my possessions to help others. I do EVERYTHING I am supposed to do! Don't You just love me, God? Look at me praying now. Isn't that nice of me?"

we pray?

The other man came quietly into the temple and stood far off not wanting anyone to see him. He bowed his head and said, "I'm not good enough to be here in God's presence! Be kind to me, God. I am a sinner!"

No one is so good that he never needs to ask God for forgiveness. Each one needs to pray, "Help me, God. I am a sinner."

The position we are in when we pray isn't important.

Some people kneel to pray; children often do, especially at bedtime.

At mealtimes, when we thank God for our food, we sit.

At church, when we talk to God with other people . . .

we sit . . .

. . . or stand.

Where should we pray?

We do not have to be in church to pray. We can pray wherever we are. God wants us to talk to Him anytime and anyplace.

Where did Jonah pray? (Jonah 2:1)

Where did Job pray?
(Job 1:20)

Where did Daniel pray?
(Daniel 6:10)

Where did Cornelius pray?
(Acts 10:30)

Where did Peter pray?
(Acts 10:9)

Where did Lydia and her friends pray? (Acts 16:13)

To Whom do we pray?

Did you ever think about what we call God in our prayers? We call Him, "Father."

That is a wonderful word! We do not have to pray by saying, "Most all-powerful ruler of the universe, may it please you to listen to the small matters of one of your subjects. . . ."

Instead we can say, "Father." We know this because Jesus gave us a "sample" prayer. It begins, "Our Father." Today we call this simple prayer, "The Lord's Prayer."

The Lord's Prayer does two things: praises and asks. The beginning and the ending of the prayer are praising. The middle part is asking.

The Lord's Prayer

Our Father which art in heaven,
Hallowed be thy name.
Thy kingdom come.
Thy will be done in earth,
as it is in heaven.
Give us this day our daily bread.
And forgive us our debts,
as we forgive our debtors.
And lead us not into temptation,
but deliver us from evil:
For thine is the kingdom,
and the power, and the glory,
for ever.
Amen.

—Matthew 6:9-13

The asking for "daily bread" reminds us that we don't need the whole bakery—just what we need for each day.

The asking for forgiveness for ourselves helps us remember to forgive others.

The asking for help to keep from doing wrong is an important part of the prayer. Jesus said, "Pray that you don't even get into places where you might think about doing wrong!"

Another time, Jesus said we should pray in His name. We can do this by saying, "In Jesus' name," at the end of our prayers. (And then, "Amen!")

"The Lord is near to all who call on him"—Psalm 145:18. (NIV)